John Randall

The Fairies' Festival

John Randall

The Fairies' Festival

ISBN/EAN: 9783743344570

Manufactured in Europe, USA, Canada, Australia, Japa

Cover: Foto ©ninafisch / pixelio.de

Manufactured and distributed by brebook publishing software (www.brebook.com)

John Randall

The Fairies' Festival

The Fairies' Festival.

The Fairies' Festival

By JOHN WITT RANDALL

EDITED BY
FRANCIS ELLINGWOOD ABBOT
ILLUSTRATED BY
FRANCIS GILBERT ATTWOOD

BOSTON
JOSEPH KNIGHT COMPANY
1895

Copyright, 1894.
By Joseph Knight Company.

BIOGRAPHICAL NOTE.

John Witt Randall, the author of this little poem, was born in Boston, November 6, 1813. His father was Dr. John Randall, a graduate of Harvard College in the class of 1802, and one of the most eminent physicians of his time in Boston; and his mother was Elizabeth (Wells) Randall, grand-daughter of Samuel Adams, the illustrious "Father of the Revolution." After receiving his preparatory education at Mr. Green's school in Jamaica Plain and at the Boston Latin School, he entered Harvard College in 1830, and was graduated in the class of 1834. Subsequently he took the degree of Doctor of Medicine at the Harvard Medical School, but never practised his profession.

At first, Dr. Randall's tastes were largely in the direction of natural history, especially entomology. His early proficiency in this field was so marked and so widely recognized that he received the appointment of "professor of zoölogy in the department of invertebrate animals" in the South Sea Exploring Expedition, generally known as "Wilkes's Expedition," which sailed from Norfolk, Virginia, on August 18, 1838. But the long delay in the starting of this expedition had exhausted his patience, and he resigned his honorable appointment just before Wilkes set sail.

From that time Dr. Randall passed his life in leisure and retirement from the world, devoting himself to the care of the family property and the indulgence of his tastes for literature, especially poetry, and the fine arts. In the course of many years, he accumulated a collection of some twenty thousand etchings and engravings, illustrating the whole history of the art and possessing a priceless value in the eyes of competent judges; and at his death, in accordance with his wishes, this precious collection and a permanent fund of thirty thousand dollars to provide for its custody and increase were given to Harvard University.

In 1856, he published at his own expense, through John P. Jewett, the original publisher of " Uncle Tom's Cabin," a modest volume of poems with the title of " Consolations of Solitude." His rooted aversion, however, to what he called "puffery," including, perhaps, quite legitimate advertisements under that name, rendered a large sale impossible, and he soon recalled the remnant of the edition for gratuitous distribution. This unconquerable but characteristic repugnance to use of the ordinary means for making his poems known prevented their reaching and pleasing many minds, if the cordial appreciation of a few choice spirits, such as Ralph Waldo Emerson, William

Cullen Bryant, Richard Henry Dana, Sr., Epes Sargent, Ephraim Peabody, and Edwin P. Whipple, afford any indication of their probable reception by a larger public.

In " Memorials of the Class of 1834, of Harvard College, prepared for the Fiftieth Anniversary of their Graduation by Thomas Cushing, at the Request of his Classmates," Dr. Randall wrote : —

" As to my literary works, — if I except scientific papers on subjects long ago abandoned, as one on Crustacea in the Transactions of the Academy of Natural Sciences, of Philadelphia ; two on Insects in the Transactions of the Boston Society of Natural History ; one manuscript volume on the Animals and Plants of Maine, furnished to Dr. Charles T. Jackson to accompany his Geological Survey of that State, and lost by him ; Critical Notes on Etchers and Engravers, one volume, and Classification of ditto, one volume, both in manuscript, incomplete and not likely to be completed, together with essays and reviews not likely to be published, — my doings reduce themselves to six volumes of poetic works, the first of which was issued in 1856 and reviewed shortly after in the *North American*, while the others, nearly or partially completed at the outbreak of the civil war, still lie unfinished among the many wrecks of Time, painful to most of us to look back upon, or reflect themselves on a Future whose skies are yet obscure."

These poetical manuscripts, in a state of confusion that

may yet baffle all attempts to recover much from them, Dr. Randall left to the editor, his younger but most intimate friend for more than forty years, to do with them whatever may prove possible. The present poem on "The Fairies' Festival" is an episode in a larger poem, entitled "Metamorphoses of Longing," which it is intended to publish hereafter as a whole, together with a revision of the "Consolations of Solitude" from the author's pencilled corrections, and several later poems not included in that early volume. How much more can be done with the almost impracticable manuscripts remains to be seen; but the works already indicated are sufficient, in the editor's hope and belief, to establish for John Witt Randall, who was himself utterly indifferent to fame, a long delayed but honorable and permanent position among American poets.

Dr. Randall was never married, and died on January 25, 1892, at the age of seventy-eight years.

THE EDITOR.

List of Illustrations.

LIST OF ILLUSTRATIONS.

	PAGE
Title Page	
First Fairy	1
Second Fairy	2
Third Fairy	2
Fourth Fairy	3
Fifth Fairy	3
Sixth Fairy	4
Seventh Fairy	4
Eighth Fairy	5
Ninth Fairy	5
Tenth Fairy	6
" Let the acorn goblet swim ".	9
" But fly to rest on greenwood boughs "	12
" Quick! the sable cloud-cloth throw "	13
" While the merry round we make "	17
" Look, where the moon her way doth wedge "	19
" Now in lengthening line once more "	21
" Lift her to yon oaken bough "	23
" Hail, flower of all our Fairy forces! "	27
First Complainant	31

LIST OF ILLUSTRATIONS.

	PAGE
Second Complainant	34
Third Complainant	34
Fourth Complainant	35
Fifth Complainant	36
"So swear we all"	39
"Set us each night beside the door"	41
"Suck their eggs"	43
"When the goody 'gins to doze"	44
"Melt in the mists of morn, and ride in wreaths away"	47
"And to flask and flagon crawl"	49
"Our merry chant of gratitude"	53
"A priest half drunk, his cowl aslouch"	57
"I've picked his corkscrew up!"	60
"Fly to the dance once more"	67
"Born to dwell with birds and flowers"	73
"For his own Bible doth confess"	81
"I love a jovial life and free"	82
"Come, every knight! Come, every Fay!"	91
"Whirl with the winds away!"	96

(THE POET DREAMS, AND HEARS FAIRIES SINGING IN THE DISTANCE.)

FIRST FAIRY.

Awhile, fair moon, delay,
   And kindly heed our longing;
We dress the woods for May,
   Our hosts are through them thronging.

SECOND FAIRY.

For us the night shall glow
    O'er grove and fount and rill;
The little Dwarfs, also,
    Shall join us from the hill.

THIRD FAIRY.

The cataract shall fall free,
    Nor toil to grind the grain;
No axe shall touch the tree,
    No plough shall fret the plain.

FOURTH FAIRY.

And let no mortal eye
  Behold our rare delight,
No mortal step draw nigh:
  To us belongs the night.

FIFTH FAIRY.

No man be near to boast
  His vain and selfish creed,
For Nature's countless host
  Takes of his power small heed.

SIXTH FAIRY.

'Tis she that doth award
    Each creature's field and house,
And views with like regard
    The mountain and the mouse.

SEVENTH FAIRY.

Glad in the bright moon's beam,
  We laugh at mortal strife;
Our duty is to dream,
  And health our aim of life.

EIGHTH FAIRY.

So let men boast their souls!
   God only knows his heirs:
He that the world controls
   Can give the Fairies theirs.

NINTH FAIRY.

Till then be it ours to enjoy,
   To dance by the firefly's lamp;
No prayer our feast alloy,
   No priest our spirits damp.

TENTH FAIRY.

Awake, ye deities of old,
Ye that have slept so long in mould;
Gather from fountain, field, and plain
Your ancient worshippers again.

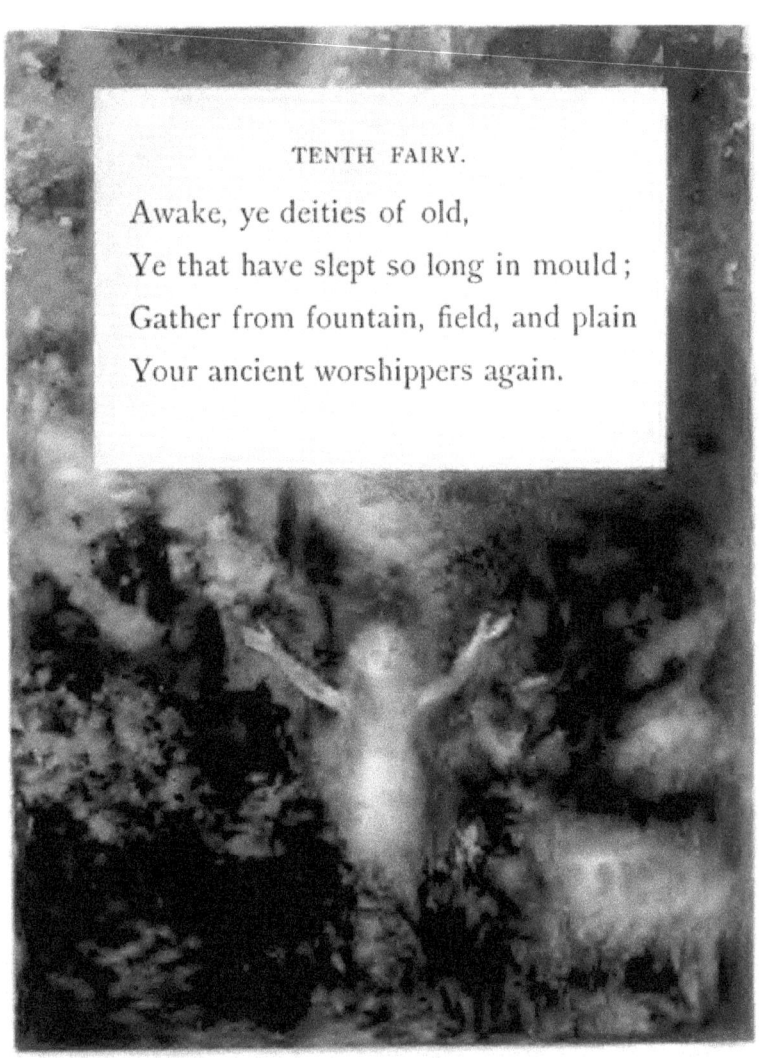

(THE DREAMER HALF WAKES.)

Hark! 'Midst the falling dew
I hear the Elfin crew!
Like rustling leaves they gently wail,
Singing together in the dale,
As when of old upon the green
They met to dance around their queen.
And now 'tis sounding far and faint,
A sweet and melancholy plaint;
Now like a rising breeze it swells,
Now vibrates like those tiny bells
That some curious Swiss hath hid
Underneath a snuff-box lid,
Whose notes fly off from tinkling steel
Like raindrops from a water-wheel;
And now a distant fall it seems,
Whose murmurings lull to sleep and dreams.

FIRST FAIRY.

Come, sisters all, come dressed in white,
We hold our annual feast to-night.
The meadow smokes with silvery haze,
The fireflies all are in a blaze:
Let us dance where daisies grow,
Till the morning cock shall crow,
And with shrilly discord scare
All of us to empty air!
Where the nodding foxglove stands,
Pluck the flowers and deck your hands;
Moth-wing each and lily bring,
One for fan and one to ring.
Fill with milk the pitchers, fill
From the blue cow on the hill
That a month on dew hath fed,
Where the springy slopes outspread,
All with green moss carpeted.
Let the acorn goblet swim,

Filled with fresh wine to the brim,
Stolen from the shopman's stall
While his clerk was at the ball.
Reindeer moss will make good cheer,
Spruce leaves fresh will brew our beer,
While cresses sweet and cranberries sound
In the meadows can be found.
When the midnight hour is past
And our tired feet fly less fast,
By the glow-worm's light we'll feast
Till the dawn hath streaked the east.
When the sky-lark doth awake
In the woodside o'er the lake,
And the mill-wheel 'gins to wail
Where the brook falls down the dale,
We no longer must carouse,
But fly to rest on greenwood boughs.

SECOND FAIRY.

But, if mortal foot
    should tread
Where our tables are
    outspread,
Let the watch-guard whistle thrice,
And at the third blast in a trice,

Fast as fire sparks swiftly shot
From the blacksmith's anvil hot,
Quick! the sable cloud-cloth throw
O'er the feast and round the foe.

Till, in inky darkness blind,
Ne'er a footpath can he find.
Vanish into air, or hie
Upon moonbeams to the sky;
There in fleecy clouds remain

Till in dews ye drop again;
Or, descending with the showers
That refresh the field and flowers,
Melt with spirits light and gay
In the mists of heaven away,
Or sink in raindrops to the ground.
Come, now for another round!

THIRD FAIRY.

Lo, our goddess, waked from sleep,
Mounts above the glowing deep!
Up the heavens behold her sail
In a silver-fringéd veil,
Casting adown her anchor bright
Into a sea of crystal light;
Till, fading in the twilight gray,
She floats in silvery mists away,
Or with the grim approach of morn

Gazes on a world forlorn,
While the blithe Fairies, hand in hand,
Unbroken yet their cheerful band,
Still half in doubt uncertain stand,
Till, lost at last when o'er the wave
She sinks within her ocean grave,
The Fairies doubt no more, but fly
As the last moonbeam leaves the sky.

FOURTH FAIRY.

Swing the harebell, sound the chime,
Tripping lightly to the time,
While the leaves on every tree
Rustle all in harmony.
Louder yet, mount, merry choirs!
Perch on twigs and grassy spires,
Make each leaf and grass-blade quake.
While the merry round we make.

" *Monday — Tuesday — Wednesday*" — hark!
Something's whirring through the dark;
A bat is out to chase a moth,
Just from her cocoon crept forth.
" *Thursday — Friday — Saturday*" — hold!
None of us must be so bold
As the next word to sing or say:
Time hath no future for the Fay!
Fly we to pleasure, not to thought —
Our world is now, the next is nought.
O woe, woe, woe! No souls have we —
The fields of Heaven we must not see,
And, when our thoughtless lives are o'er,
We sleep in death to wake no more.

FIFTH FAIRY.

Look, where the moon her way doth wedge
Through yon gray cloud's glittering edge!

She struggles hard — now
    lift your eyes —
She's out, and through the
    starry skies
            Swims cheerily, and now she gleams
            On us with a hundred beams.

SIXTH FAIRY.

Methinks the wind begins to rise;
How fast each flickering shadow flies,
Wheeling like us in many a maze!
Up, up again, up, sister Fays!
The days are long, and night is fleet.
Swiftly trip with tinkling feet;
Now one by one, now two by two,
Clear the grass, but spare the dew;
Now three by three, now four by four,
Swift as a cataract we pour;
Now in lengthening line once more,
Now five, six, seven, in wreathéd chain,
Whirl like wheels, and whirl again;
While the boughs and leaves around
Dance in shadows on the ground,
Leap from shade to shade — be fleet —
Who touches light shall wet her feet.
"*Monday — Tuesday — Wednesday*" hist!

Something's whirring
 through the mist;
The owl's on wing to
 seize a mouse
That peeps from yon
 deserted house.
" *Thursday — Friday —*
 Saturday" — cease!
Shun the name that
 breaks our peace.
No souls have we —
 woe ne'er forgot!
Who knows if we have
 souls or not?
Alas, I fear we have
 our day,
Then like the flowers
 must fade away.

SEVENTH FAIRY.

Moon and stars are glowing bright,
All the world is ours to-night;
Be we beauteous while we may!
Short the night and long the day,
And dawn shall send us all to bed
With pallid cheeks and eyelids red.

ALL THE FAIRIES IN CHORUS.

Here our Queen comes! Crown her brow,
Lift her to yon oaken bough:
On every twig, from every leaf,
Hail with songs your Fairy Chief!
Let the bands with might and main
Pipe through straws the reedy strain!
Hark! I hear the hunter's horn
Sounding from yon field of corn,
Whence our huntsmen to the ring
In long array come galloping,

In kirtles green and caps of red,
And some with crystals helmeted,
That flash their light in dazzling rays
And crown each warrior with a blaze.
Hail, flower of all our Fairy forces!
Mounted all on milk-white horses,
With milk-white tails that stream behind
Shining and fluttering in the wind,
Like a river o'er a rock
Beat to white foam by the shock,
Climbing now the steep hillside,
In what a merry troop ye ride!
And the music jangling swells
From a thousand silver bells,
While through the whistles in their manes
The air breathes in delicious strains.

QUEEN.

Welcome, knights from near and far,
Whencesoe'er ye gathered are!
See, o'er all our magic ground
Every bush with Fays is crowned,
To every bough and twig we cling,
The trees with us are blossoming!
Sip our dew and share our cheer;
None but friends are gathered here;
No evil beast, no bird of night,
Shall come hither to affright;
Gladly will you guard your Queen
With bulrush sharp and flag-blade keen
If too curious maid or man
Seek our secret rites to scan,
Wandering hither from the hill,
Warn them thrice by whistles shrill:
Light the bog-lamps where they tread,
Trembling, o'er the marshy bed, —

Where the swamp-holes, scattered round,
Feign resemblance to a mound,
And Will-o'-wisp in sportive play
Tempts them from their path astray, —
Where the greenest of all grass
Scantly hides the deep morass,
And the gold-thread, grouped in bowers,
Cheats the eye with seeming flowers.
Now let us hold our annual court;
Let words be few and stories short.
Speak — and, if mortal man or maid
Hath made any Fay afraid
In the villages about,
Whether in the house or out,
Clipping wings or in the street
Setting traps to catch their feet,
Placing food on hearth or floor
With rat-poison smearéd o'er,
Or pricking melons for their ill

With emetic, draught, or pill,
Or making window-sash with springs
Prone to fall and crush their wings,
When they climb for trifling cheer
To sip a drop of milk or beer,
Now tell the wrong, that there be sent
On their heads just punishment.
Now swear ye all!

    FAIRIES IN CHORUS.

                So swear we all,
Dire vengeance on their heads shall fall!
But nay — a moment wait — not yet,
Or the chief boon we shall forget!
Therefore, we first of all demand
That all their priests, in solid band,
Shall of their gods a blessing pray
On the whole race of Dwarf and Fay
And furnish souls for all our Elves —
Just such as those they wear themselves!

QUEEN.

The claim is just, and here I stand
Sworn to amend our late demand.
Now swear again, swear all!

FAIRIES IN CHORUS.

           We swear,
Such shall the Fairies' friendship share!

QUEEN.

Now speak, if any have a grief,
And, if we can, we'll give relief.

FIRST COMPLAINANT.

I asked the old maids at Donald's Head
To give me a small piece of bread;
They caught me up, and stuck my shin
Into the dough and baked me in.

SECOND COMPLAINANT.

Me to a spider's web they tied
Was woven on the window side;
Within the web a hornet hung,
And, while I struggled, I was stung.

THIRD COMPLAINANT.

A goody promised me an egg,
If I would only seven pence beg
To buy a plaster for her leg,
And, when I brought all I could get,
A rotten one for me she set,
And, while I tried to
  break the shell,
It burst and blew me
  down the well.

FOURTH COMPLAINANT.

'Twas but next day her bad good-man
Caught me, too, at the dairy pan.
"What dost thou there?" says he. Says I:
"Good Sir, I hungry am and dry."
Then from the meat pot he drew forth
A bowl full of hot mutton broth,
And put me in. The broth grew cool,
And held me like a frozen pool.
He set us both upon a shelf,
And said: "Now drink thy fill, poor Elf!"
There through the long night did I flout,
Till the kind mice could eat me out.

FIFTH COMPLAINANT.

A beldam took me for a rat,
And straightway threw me to the cat.
The cat, being old, had lost her spirit,
Which I did even through youth inherit;
So up I stood and stroked her fur,
When presently she began to purr,
And licked my hands, and we were friends.
Cold mutton broth had made amends
For all disgust; she licked me clean,
All sweet and savory to be seen,
And fit to stand before my Queen.

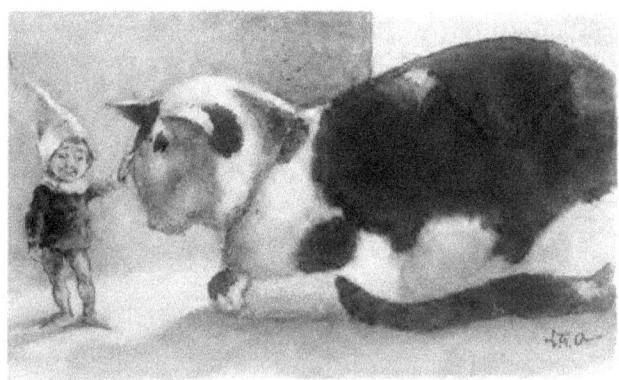

QUEEN.

Of all the sentiments expressed
The cats and dogs hold still the best —
Death and the Devil may take the rest!
These people, until they mend their ways,
Shall brook the vengeance of the Fays,
And, since even beasts have learned to prize
Those kindly acts which men despise,
Let us be kind to them even more
Than we were kind to men before.
Now swear ye all!

FAIRIES IN CHORUS.

So swear we all,
Dire vengeance on our foes shall fall!
They shall meet a recompense
In famine, fire, and pestilence.
In the unerring hand of Fate,
Little things are oft most great;

Justice rules alike o'er all,
Whether they be great or small.
A Queen who guards and still defends,
Who treats her subjects as her friends,
And to her foes need never yield
In secret wile or open field,
Is one we love! Then bid us stand,
All proud to follow thy command
And serve thee still.

QUEEN.

                Our time we bide!
Let none despond, let none deride:
Vengeance, however slow or late,
Drops like the unswerving bolt of Fate,
Which falls unseen with lightning speed
And smites in one both thought and deed.
Such be the doom of every foe
To our proud race — a word and blow!

Yet, if among them all, so free
To boast their Christian charity,
Some few there be would show by deeds
The faith on which their self-love feeds,
And, fain to share with us their store,
Set us each night beside the door,
Of all the good things baked or boiled,
Some scanty portion ere 'tis spoiled,

Of tithes the thousandth part, and beer
Through the deep bog our steps to steer,
And in cold winter nights the hashes
Set by the fire or on the ashes,
With just a drop of gin or ale
To keep us steady in the dale —
One acorn-cup each night, no more, —
Then swear, as each did swear before,
We'll friend with such, both maid and man,
And do them all the good we can.

FAIRIES, IN PART.

But the unfriendly ought to feel
Vengeance more sharp than foeman's steel.

QUEEN.

Swear, then, to plague them through the year!
Suck their eggs and sour their beer,
Steal their milk and craze their dogs,

Poison all their cows and hogs.
When the goody 'gins to doze,
Hold a match beneath her nose;
Go, Fairy Incubus, at night,
Fill her goodman's dreams with fright,
Mount his belly while abed,
Lying like a load of lead,
Till he wakes with sudden scare,
Clutching the fiend, to clench the air.
Such full oft, amidst their moan,
Have some fearful crime made known;
Thus many a thief and murderer caught

To the gallows hath been brought;
Nay, some, though guiltless, have confessed
The crimes that slept within the breast
Unrecognized, till some still hour
When conscience wakes with sudden power,
And a winged dream's unconscious flight

Hath brought the error to the light,
And made them in their drowsy state
The ministers of their own fate.
But we lose time, and time is pleasure,
The only duty we can measure.
Come, Fairies, it is wearing late,
Your knights around impatient wait;
This is the festival of May,
Sacred alike to every Fay.
Now let our feet, like falling rain,
Lightly patter on the plain;
And, when in one brief hour
Fatigue shall end the shower,
Then feast we till the approach of day.
First pales the moon, then let each knight and Fay
Melt in the mists of morn, and ride in wreaths away.
Now, merry knights and laughing Elves,
Who so happy as ourselves?
On our frames pain hath no hold,

We can bear both heat and cold,
And, while we live, each moonlit night
Shall yield us many a dear delight,
Wheresoe'er we dance, the scene
Ever glows with livelier green,
In freshest youth our lives we spend,
But feel no sorrow at the end.

NINTH FAIRY.

While with famine cities pine,
We can filch both bread and wine,
Through the pantry wire-screen creep,
When the maids are fast asleep,
And to flask and flagon crawl
Through the chink of cellar wall,
Then to the forest with our prize,
Ere the cook hath rubbed her eyes.
We, the sordid priest to pay
For his hatred of the Fay,

All unseen can mount the stairs
While the monks are at their prayers,
And with their golden crowns make free,
Robbing the chest without the key.
In life delighting while 'twill last,
We hail no future, mourn no past,

And, when we die, no grieving train
Bears us to the funeral wain,
Nor in death-vaults, damp and cold,
Do we rot like meaner mould.
Locked together arm in arm,
We pass away without alarm;
Gently vanishing in air,
We go, we know not when or where,
And what we are, or whither go,
We care as little as we know.

QUEEN.

Yet deem we not that, when we fade,
We are doomed to darksome shade,
Nor through vacant space to fly
Without moon or stars or sky.
He who moulds that purer earth
Whence our blithesome race had birth
Is not likely to employ

His wise skill but to destroy,
Stamp His own image but to excite
A transient feeling of delight,
And, as our grateful thanks ascend,
Even break the die He cannot mend.
Nay, He enjoys, if He be good,
Our merry chant of gratitude.
Deem not the All-pervading Power
That life inspires in field and flower,
Whose joy is but in giving breath,
Can e'er delight in endless death.
He still, though without souls, can give
Us grateful Fays the right to live.
Such is the Deity we bless,
Who doth a kingly soul possess —
He who, on some clear Christmas night,
Made our sires from moonbeams bright,
While upon our birth from far
Softly smiled each twinkling star,

Which, when Diana bears her bow
With her crescent on her brow,
Even yet in heaven delights to shine
And bless her progeny divine,
When we, the loveliest of her train,
Dance upon the glittering plain,
And make with songs and pastime gay
Our nights far happier than man's day
Nor are we doomed amongst the dead
To lie with worms in loathsome bed.
When the goddess chaste and fair
Melts our forms again to air,
If to us she hath not given
Entrance to the gates of Heaven,
When our life's last moon hath set,
She at least will soothe regret
And allow us to forget.
Till then we have no further care;
Whate'er we have, we freely share;

No joy in self alone doth end —
Mate gives to mate, and friend to friend;
In greenest youth our lives we pass.

FAIRIES IN CHORUS.

If only we had souls, alas!
Sing sadly, all our hopes are fled:
Man shall survive when we are dead.
"*Monday — Tuesday — Wednesday — Thursday —
Friday — Saturday*"— try once more.
"*Monday — Tuesday — Wednesday — Thursday —
Friday — Saturday*" — hold, give o'er;
The next we must not sing nor say:
We have our joys — but, while we play,
Our hapless souls are stolen away.

TENTH FAIRY.

For one, I'll bear to do without;
As to their worth, I'm much in doubt.

I cannot say, but yet I deem
That those things are not what they seem —
Almost I fear, an empty dream.
What knave so pious as a man?
He prays, but ever hath a plan,
And in his seeming we can see
Only long-faced hypocrisy.
But hark! what noise is yonder?   Hush!
Some one is jogging through the bush.
I smell a priest, his ass astride,
With a flagon at his side —
A flagon large, a bible small —
The latter he hath just let fall —
A priest half drunk, his cowl aslouch,
And a prayer-book in his pouch.
In yonder town, all scant of breath,
Two spinsters lie at point of death —
At point of death impatient wait
To get a passport through Heaven's gate.

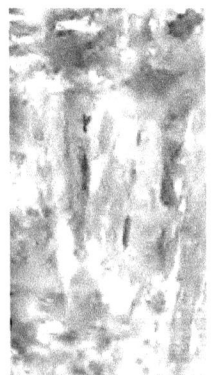

ELEVENTH FAIRY.

I smell him strong outside our ring:
Let's run, and to his skirt-flaps cling!

FAIRIES (*pursuing him*).

Ho, priest! Ho, priest! We fain would know
If Fairies must their souls forego;
And, if we have them, can you tell
Whether we're doomed to Heaven or Hell?
What says he? That he hath "forgot
Whether we have souls or not!"

TWELFTH FAIRY.

I'll chase him, for methinks his soul
Hath soaked full long in yonder bowl.

FAIRIES (*pursuing*).

Ho, priest! Thy fervent prayers we crave,
Such as have power the lost to save!

THIRTEENTH FAIRY.

Give us a good drink from thy can,
To breed us souls like that in man!

FOURTEENTH FAIRY.

And a pass to Heaven, while you're about it!
If such a place be, though I doubt it.

FIFTEENTH FAIRY.

Alas, poor man, I fear the gin
Hath drowned what soul he had within.

SIXTEENTH FAIRY.

I've picked his corkscrew up! No doubt,
The thing could draw his secret out.

SEVENTEENTH FAIRY.

Good Father, wait a little, do,
And give us Fairies passports, too!
And may a thousand years have flown
Or ever you shall need your own!

FAIRIES (*all chasing him*).

Stop, priest! Stop, ass! Why fly so fast?
The fellow travels like a blast.

EIGHTEENTH FAIRY.

Nay, nay, no more! Full far they've flown;
I seized his frock and tore my own.

NINETEENTH FAIRY.

I chased him hard, and pulled the rein,
And begged he'd pray for us — 'twas vain!

TWENTIETH FAIRY.

I clutched the ass's tail — see there —
All that I got this tuft of hair!

TWENTY-FIRST FAIRY.

And now we're left in grief and doubt!
If we have souls, we can't find out.

QUEEN.

I hear the click from clock-tower gray;
Listen, and hear what it will say.
"*Ding, dong! Ding, dong! One — two — three — four!*"
I hear the distant thunder roar.
"*Ding, dong! Ding, dong! Five — six — seven — eight!*"
Fairies, the eve is wearing late.
"*Ding, dong! Ding, dong!*" But two hours more,
And feast and dance must both be o'er;
The Nameless Day must come at last,
And all our pleasure shall be past.

SIXTH FAIRY.

List! What voices from the dell
Hither through the greenwood swell,
Voices loud and footsteps fleet,
Words which yonder rocks repeat?
The village surgeon's on the road
And the rich lawyer, both abroad
Summoned in haste and quickly sped
To reach the house at Donald's Head,
Where the sick spinsters patient wait
To mount the black coach for Heaven's gate.
If the Devil in league with Death
Are not enough to stop their breath,
The Squire and Doctor will compete
To make the half-done job complete.
If, like his ass, his head were steady,
The half-dazed Priest were there already
And, when they all are met together,
I'll pledge my Fairy cap-and-feather,

The crones will die, to 'scape the curse
Of all the three — a fate that's worse!
Of writs and pills and prayers all blent,
'Twill make the spinsters well content
To join the dust from whence they went —
For thither, whatsoe'er his creed,
Man must go back the worms to feed.

SEVENTH FAIRY.

The worms to feed? How hard the fate,
If God did really man create,
To live for aye in such a state —
Beneath this dreadful doom to be
Through ages of eternity!
Surely some pity we must feel,
Even though our hearts were hard as steel,
And, were we but of Heaven the heirs,
Man should not fail to have the prayers
Of our whole race! But, ah, the Elves

Have promise of no souls themselves,
And we, being doomed to endless sleep,
For him can nothing do but weep.
Our tears would never change his state:
Let us even leave him to his fate.
This is the sole means we, poor Elves,
Can even escape despair ourselves.
Fly to the dance once more,
Yet merrier than before!
Brief our time, and daylight soon
Shall scare away the stars and moon.
Be we beauteous while we may —
Brief the night and long the day!
When the thrush at morning sings,
We must shrink to common things.
Smiling o'er the world's repose,
For us alone fair Evening glows;
Alone we know the dear delight
Born of wakefulness and night.

Careless we as summer flowers —
Man no pleasure hath like ours.
We can laugh while he must weep;
We can wake while he must sleep,
Or brood all night on coming sorrow:
What care night-birds for the morrow?
He by poverty is vexed —
We are by no wants perplexed;
He, though tired, must toil all day —
We of nothing tire but play;
While he frets o'er public ills,
We in freedom roam the hills,
Or lie down midst breezes cool
In the grot or by the pool,
Or dream the hours in solemn shade
On the hill or in the glade.
— But listen, sisters, for I hear
The hearse of Death approaching near.
And Death's pale coachman, lean as he,

Wrapped up upon the front I see,
And in his mouth the pipe is lighted,
And, that he may not grow benighted,
The weed, that every moment glows,
Lights up the roadway as he goes.
The sisters hope some brief delay,
One half hour with the Priest to pray,
To mend the reading of their will
Drawn by the Lawyer's clerkly skill,
To gulp the Doctor's bitter stuff, —
Then both of life will cry enough,
And long for pickaxe and for spade
To lay them in the darksome shade.
Yet boots it not; this night they die,
While the south wind is rising high.
But one hour more!   The midnight bell
Shall sound their death, and with the knell
They must be doomed to Heaven or Hell.

QUEEN.

We have no souls at worst — at best
We should be hopeful, like the rest.
Naught is more foolish than despair!
Much have we borne, and more can bear:
Why should we dread for aye to sleep?
'Tis better than to wake and weep!
Man is daily doomed to mourn,
Even as the sparks are upward borne,
Grieving still, in cot and hall,
O'er the daily funeral,
Or the torments that await
Mortals in the future state,
Where his dead friends, gone before,
Wait him on some dismal shore.
Our lily-cup and blue harebell
Never sound the sad death-knell;
And, if beyond this life our race
May never know a happier place,

Still 'tis a comfort not to be
Doomed to the mortal's destiny.
This our sole grief — we cannot know
Or what we are or whither go.
On our frames pain hath no hold,
We can scorn both hot and cold,
We can live long and not grow old;
And he who trusts us, even mankind,
Will ever faithful service find.
Born to dwell with birds and flowers,
There is no happiness like ours,
And, while our own is unforgot,
All other bliss we envy not.
We have no need of surgeon's skill;
Fever heat and ague chill
Fasten not on us; our day
Knows not faintness nor decay,
Nor hath consumption cold the power
To cut us off in life's first flower;

Nor are we racked by pains of gout,
Nor doth dread asthma find us out :
In greenest youth our lives we pass —
'Tis only souls we lack, alas!
All other pain we can assuage
From earliest infancy to age,
And, when our joyous lives are past,
We sink to dreamless sleep at last.
Sing sadly, all our hope is fled :
Man shall survive when we are dead!

TWELFTH FAIRY.

Now the old tale I call to mind
That we were once of angel kind,
And 'mongst the rebel angels fell,
Though not, like them, condemned to Hell, —
But still to live, such was our fate,
In the degraded Fairy state.
But since 'twas man alone, not we,

That robbed fair Eden's apple tree,
O why was not our race forgiven,
And left some scanty share of Heaven?
Is it for this we live forlorn?
Is it for this we ceaseless mourn?
Ah, careless of the Fairy's fate,
There's none bewails our soulless state!
And, when we tell our hopes and fears,
We get but curses for our tears!
To pray for us no stupid monk
Will deign, however mad or drunk;
No guardian angel will descend
To be the hapless Fairy's friend;
No Son of God, no saint e'er gave
His life to lift us from the grave;
But, when our aimless lives are o'er,
We sleep in death and wake no more!

QUEEN.

And is there one of us so mean
As on another's staff would lean?
'Tis but a coward that would pack
His burden on another's back;
Nay, let the almighty hand of Fate
Even our whole race annihilate,
Ere we be false to honor's laws!
That will not justify our cause;
He who from honor's laws has swerved
May deem his loss of soul deserved!
Leave fraud to man, who never spares,
But acts the tyrant where he dares.
Nay, shall the innocent atone
For crimes that never were their own?
I would not that the meanest life
Should bleed for mine beneath the knife,
Nor that one drop of blood be spilt
To drown the memory of my guilt,

Nor that the sword or axe or stake
Should e'er claim victims for my sake —
Not even the lambs or birds we cherish;
And, sure, far less that God should perish —
God, who made the world so vast,
And made it strong enough to last,
And wisely made, so firm and sure
That it forever might endure,
That all His creatures might be free
To worship through eternity!
'Tis mutual love that cheers our night
And makes our hearts and steps so light;
One selfish wish our bond would sever,
And Fairy hopes were lost forever.
'Tis true, we cannot change our state,
But let us ne'er deserve our fate;
Let God forever in our eyes
Seem just as kind, and good as wise!

NINTH FAIRY.

Gods of the priest, benignant list,
Pity our sorrows and assist!
Good Lord, good Devil, lend an ear,
If either have the power to hear —
If neither, let it end the fuss;
The devil a prayer you'll get from us.
Witches and Fairies are ill starred;
The gates of Heaven 'gainst both are barred,
And then comes doom without relief.
These words I heard with pain and grief,
These very words, without a doubt
From the church windows streaming out,
As on the grass outstretched I lay,
Half waking, on the Nameless Day: —
" A witch thou never shalt forgive,
Nor even suffer her to live!"
Hater of good that God must be
Who is misfortune's enemy —

Whose ear, in palace or in hut,
Can to true penitence be shut!
'Tis worse than useless to complain
Of what we are and must remain;
Yet, when he said good works were nought
And but the worse damnation brought,
" If but the bad are saved," thought I,
" The rest are happiest when they die!
The bad alone are saved, though few;
Such only can be born anew.
Rather than hope for such a Heaven,
Hopeless I'd live — die unforgiven!"

TENTH FAIRY.

Nay, nay, good sister! 'Tis not wise
Ever, like man, to moralize.
Ere long you'll say 'tis wrong to steal,
And fatal to the common weal!
But, sister, 'twill not do to trace

Our likeness to the human race,
For this, as long as time shall roll,
Will never save a Fairy soul.
'Tis true we steal from man, but he
Is to our race an enemy;
While in himself this fault we find —
He hath no mercy for his kind!
Though all are brethren named, we see
'Tis nothing but hypocrisy;
Which if you doubt, just read the book
That from the flying priest we took,
For his own Bible doth confess,
Man's works are nought but filthiness!
But we as brethren really bide;
We love each other, nothing hide,
What each one hath we all divide.
That is true innocence which dreads,
Not darkened nights, but evil deeds;
Hence darkness never do we fear,

Nor dread we night when it is near;
The darkest nights, for sport and play,
To us are but as brightest day.

And this is why we so delight
In starry eve and moonlight bright:
'Tis innocence that makes us gay,
And chases every fear away.

ELEVENTH FAIRY.

I love a jovial life and free,
I scorn an innocent to be!
To pilfer is the Fairy's fate —
That of the parson is to prate.

Yet surely no small risk we run
Of being disabled for our fun,
And all we gain of corn and beer
Will scarce suffice the night to cheer,
Ere warning comes from chanticleer!
That must we heed with earliest day,
And slight the sport, and soar away,
Or we ourselves might make a feast
For famished bird or prowling beast,
More dangerous than a drunken priest.
A warning this that Dwarf and Fay,
Soon as they hear, must needs obey,
Nor for a single instant wait,
Unless to meet a harder fate.
I hear the click from clock-tower gray;
Listen, and hear what it will say:—
" Ding, dong! Ding, dong! One — two — three — four!"
I hear without the south wind roar.
" Ding, dong! Ding, dong! Five — six — seven — eight!"

The rain-cloud rides at rapid rate.
"*Ding, dong! Ding, dong! Nine — ten — eleven!*"
One hour is all the time that's given:
One little hour is all remains,
Though we care not how hard it rains.
Yet, though we care not for the blast
That from the south is hurrying fast,
In one brief hour the Nameless Morn
Shall come, although in darkness born;
And then each maiden and her knight
Must mount on high in rapid flight —
Must on the rushing tempest flee,
Oblivious all of gayety,
The feast, the song, the dance, the jest
Forgot alike by host and guest,
Throughout unmeasured space to fly
And make no halt — except to die!

ELEVENTH FAIRY TO TWELFTH.

Whatever truth may haply dwell
In the old story that you tell,
I doubt not that, if God could bend
To own a mortal as a friend,
As once with Abraham of old,
Then (if it might not seem too bold,
And if 'twere done with good intent)
Man might return the compliment.
But think of God, the great Unknown,
Wearing man's portrait as his own!
Is there, of all of us, an Elf
Would do the same thing for herself,
Or would consent to wear the shape
Ridiculous of man or ape?
Even though he did it, could we Elves
Play such a satire on ourselves?
Nay, even we Fairies could not find
A ruler suited to our mind,

Who for a moment, even, could wear
Our laughing eyes and flowing hair!
All save our beauteous Queen, and she
The fairest of the fair must be —
And, as in shape a head more tall,
So is she wisest of us all.

QUEEN.

O, sisters, think how wondrous far
It were to reach the nearest star!
A thousand years of ceaseless flight
Would scarcely make it seem more bright,
And, if we add ten thousands more,
As far and faint would seem the shore!
Yet, even then, we still should stand
Safe in God's all-protecting hand.
The great Inscrutable! Can He
Omniscient and all-present be
For less than all eternity?

FAIRIES IN CHORUS (*delighted*).

O Queen, your voice this moonless night
Speaks to our hearts! We feel you're right.
Henceforth how can we fail to bend
To God as Father and as Friend?

TENTH FAIRY.

O what a brief and dreary life
Fate grants these sons of toil and strife!
They cannot learn, like us, the good
Of an all-loving brotherhood.
Our feasts and songs and dances gay
Make night more happy than man's day,
And each, without a thought or plan,
Makes all as happy as she can.
Fate, when our last long moon has set
At least allows us to forget,
To fade like rainbows fair, nor crave
To learn if we have souls to save;

But when, commingling with the dead,
Men share with worms their loathsome bed,
The day which melts our forms in air
With them doth but begin despair,
For they, in fiery furnace tried,
Must first be purged and purified.

QUEEN.

O Fairies, would you change your fate
For the delights of such a state?
Nay, nay, we well might burst with laughter,
In pity of man's bright Hereafter!
O no, our blithesome Fairy race
But vanishes, and leaves no trace
In the dull clod of life's decay;
It mounts unseen and soars away,
And how, or when, or where it goes,
It asks not of its friends or foes,
And cares as little as it knows.

And would you change this for the doom
To gain damnation and a tomb?
O sisters, let us never dread
Evil from Him who reigns o'erhead,
Who ne'er one moment shall suspend
The work of Father and of Friend,
But kindly stoops the earth to bless,
Parent of life and happiness!

FAIRIES IN CHORUS (*delighted*).

O Queen, your words how can we doubt?
They drive the fiends of darkness out,
They teach us love and hope and peace,
They bid each doubt and murmur cease.
Who now can deem that God decoys
The sinner whom His wrath destroys?
In this sure truth henceforth we rest:
The greatest power is still the best!

Now for another round — the last
That we shall make or ere the blast
Shall drive us from the woods away.
Come, every knight!   Come, every Fay!
Let all move sprightly in the dance,
For this will be your latest chance,
Until a long, long year is fled,
When all of us who are not dead
Again may in these shades appear,
And dance — mayhap — another year!

TWELFTH FAIRY.

Another year!   And who will be
Alive beneath this greenwood tree?
Sisters, if any one survive
To dance beneath this tree alive,
'Tis happy that our Fairy race
Have small regard to time and place —
That, as each life doth reach its end,

Each Fairy takes another friend,
And for the old one doth not weep
Longer than o'er one fallen asleep!
And yet the new one, like the old,
She warmly loves till life is cold.
Each flutters still from flower to flower,
Feeling the rapture of the hour,
Nor deems it wisdom to lament
One moment because life is spent,
But leaves her dead friend to His care
Who planted order everywhere —
Who sends the sunshine and the rain,
And ne'er made anything in vain.
Each for herself, and God for all,
Safe in His hands, we cannot fall;
Thus they who have no souls to save
Make little mourning o'er the grave.
Even though we live a thousand years,
There's no occasion for our tears,

Since He who made us what we are
Knows best what we can do or bear.
Like man, He made us from the dust,
Nor need we doubt His doom is just.
But this, at least, is understood;
We cannot change it if we would,
And would not, even if we could.
He bade us love, and not lament,
And love the more with this intent,
That death may seem no punishment.
Thus do we all His law fulfil,
And bless the hand that holds us still,
That gives us neither toil nor task —
And more than this we dare not ask.
Seek but His worship to express
And in His will to acquiesce.
The dance is o'er, the spell is past:
In smoke our souls shall end at last!

List, what loud and sudden crash
Followed yon sharp lightning flash!
I hear the click from clock-tower gray —
Listen, and hear what it will say: —
"*Ding, dong! Ding, dong! One — two — three — four!*"
Louder the thunder 'gins to roar.
"*Ding, dong! Ding, dong! Five — six — seven — eight!*"
The storm clouds ride at rapid rate.
"*Ding, dong! Ding, dong! Cling, clang!*"   'Tis past —
The wind hath risen to a blast —
I hear the rain descending fast.
And now the convent bells are tolling,
The funeral train comes hither rolling.
List to the thunder's awful crash,
Mark the lightning's furious flash!

QUEEN.

Change, horse and knight, to feathery furze,
Ye maids, be floating gossamers!

Some to the green wood, some to the gray,
Change some to mist, and some to spray,
While some on lightning's flash whirl with
the winds away!

www.ingramcontent.com/pod-product-compliance
Lightning Source LLC
Chambersburg PA
CBHW031406160426
43196CB00007B/922